Dreams And Gibes

Edward Sapir

Nabu Public Domain Reprints:

You are holding a reproduction of an original work published before 1923 that is in the public domain in the United States of America, and possibly other countries. You may freely copy and distribute this work as no entity (individual or corporate) has a copyright on the body of the work. This book may contain prior copyright references, and library stamps (as most of these works were scanned from library copies). These have been scanned and retained as part of the historical artifact.

This book may have occasional imperfections such as missing or blurred pages, poor pictures, errant marks, etc. that were either part of the original artifact, or were introduced by the scanning process. We believe this work is culturally important, and despite the imperfections, have elected to bring it back into print as part of our continuing commitment to the preservation of printed works worldwide. We appreciate your understanding of the imperfections in the preservation process, and hope you enjoy this valuable book.

Dreams and Gibes

BY
EDWARD SAPIR

BOSTON
THE POET LORE COMPANY
THE GORHAM PRESS

COPYRIGHT, 1917, BY EDWARD SAPIR

All Rights Reserved

811.4
S239d

716235

Epitaph of a Philosopher appeared in *The Roycroft Anthology*
The Moth in *The Minaret*. They are here reproduced
through the courtesy of these magazines.

The Gorham Press, Boston, U.S.A.

TO
MY WIFE

CONTENTS

	PAGE
The Mislabeled Menagerie	9
Monks in Ottawa	11
The Builders	12
The Blind Man	13
The Old Man	14
The Man of Letters	15
The Professor	16
The Metaphysician	16
Epitaph of a Philosopher	17
The Clergyman	18
The Learned Jew	20
The Woman on the Bridge	22
To a Maiden Sweet and Pure	23
The Stenographer	24
To a Recruiting Girl	26
Professors in War-Time	27
How Diplomats Make War	28
Epitaph of a Soldier	30
The Old Maid and the Private	30
Delilah	32
The Reporter Congratulates the Orator	34
The Painting	34
The Dainty and the Hungry Man	35
The Water Nymph	38
Curtains	43
My Boy	45
Dandelions	46
The Other Side	47
Mutual Understanding	49
A Conversation	50
The Dreamer Fails of Success	50

	PAGE
Discords	53
Love	54
Our Love	55
Dangling Corpses	56
To Debussy	57
Dirty Spring	58
An Easter Day	59
Summer in the Woods	60
Before the Storm	62
A Moonless Night	62
The Rain	63
Water	63
The Moth	64
Helpless Revolt	64
Liberty	65
Dust	66
Wings	66
Loneliness	67
Vexation	68
Snared	69
The Soul	70
A Prayer for Preservation	72

DREAMS AND GIBES

THE MISLABELED MENAGERIE

I took a trip to the menagerie
To see the bear, opossum, kangaroo,
Rhinoceros and elephant, and all
My other friends whom oft I'd wondered at
Behind their bars. They're fascinating things
To gaze upon—each seems a perfect symbol
Incarnate of human virtue or of vice
Or oftenest of mirth-compelling foible.
That's why I look at them as medicine.
Just think your social-climbing friend
Who leaves you in the lurch as nimbly he jumps
From eminence to eminence until
He loses sight of you down in the valley,
Just think him carcassed in a kangaroo—
Are you revenged or not? and would you change
With him? That's why I think zoology
Is worth one's serious while—it soothes the nerves.

Hold on, I'm getting off the track; I started
To tell you how I went to see my friends
Of the menagerie. And first the bear
I visited, but in his den, if den
You'd call it, I beheld a monkey frisk
And scamper round as though the label, *Ursus*,
Were meant for him, so much at home he seemed.
I moved on to the ostrich cage and saw
A camel gravely chew the cud and squint
At me as though to say, "Too bad, my friend,
About that ostrich label. Were he you,
He'd stick his head in the sand, thus deftly
Annihilate the label, and his peace
Of ostrich mind regain." An Orient look
Of wisdom spread along the camel's face.

And when I came to where I'd always seen
The tiger nobly lash his tail and found
A fox ignobly point his tail to earth,
I knew I'd come to Topsyturvydom.
The elephant was labeled ass, the ass
Had grown a mane and pair of lion's ears—
Or so the label gravely said,—the lion
Had shrunk, it seemed, into a porcupine.

"A fussing pedagogue, no doubt, has tried
His hand," I thought, "on some new labeling
    scheme."
Just then I met a keeper. "What's the trouble,
    friend?"
I asked, "these labels are all wrong." "Oh, well,"
Said he, "we only moved the animals
This morning, and we've not got round as yet
To move the labels. We'll attend to that."

Discomfited, I turned to go, and mused
Upon my way. I ran my human friends
All through the label gauntlet and a flash—
Like Archimedes' famed Eureka—flamed
Across my mind. Why, yes, mislabeled all!
Mislabeled all! The grocer—was he not
A sturdy disputant in politics?
His label should have "statesman" been, no less.
The mayor—hard to say, but I've no doubt
That "grocer" would have served. Of clergymen
I know, two should have "broker" called themselves
And one just "simpleton." "Philanthropist"
Is just the word, or should be, for the soul
That comes each month to buy my rags and bottles,
A starving tender-hearted wretch. And so
With all the rest of them—mislabeled all!

MONKS IN OTTAWA

Right on the busy street I saw them—
Two big fat hulking plodding forms,
Strangely stuck in the hurly-burly
Like creeping flies in seething amber.
They jostled the present—
Clank of trolley-cars,
Lumbering whir of autos skidding past,
Mincing French-heeled girls with brown porous stockings
Coquettishly ribboned between petticoat and shoes,
Newsboys,
A crowd seeking fulfilment of hope from the news bulletin,
Catastrophic pictures stuck in front of the movie theatres—
They jostled the present,
They smelt of the past,
Plodding on imperturbably.

And when my eye first caught them,
"Mother of God!" said something within me,
"Holy, holy! Bosh perhaps, but holy!
Ascetic purity and mystic contemplation,
Prayer, flagellation!
St. Francis of Assisi,
God, Church, Pope, candles, faith!"
And when I came up close—
They looked like pregnant women
Wrapped in heavy brown robes,
Wearing sandals,
And I got a glimpse of a heavy silver crucifix
Tortured with crude suffering—
I heard them mumbling in their rumbling voices—
Aux champignons I fancied I could disentangle—
And they were munching peanuts.

THE BUILDERS

With confident smile, robust, clean-limbed
Of soul, you see the world as a jumble
Of millions of little blocks that have tumbled from
    their places
Or have not tumbled into them;
And you, and others clean-limbed like yourself,
Roll up your sleeves and spade them up in heaps
And disentangle them one by one,
Then carefully you place each block square to its
    neighbor
And rear up palaces.
They're never finished, for the wind and hail and
    rain
Will mock at them.
You do your best to keep them in repair,
What little time you have left over from the spad-
    ing of more blocks.

I like your ruined palaces—
A little angular perhaps—
I cannot but like them when I see you,
Confidently smiling, robust, clean-limbed of soul,
Bending in pride over them.
And yet my eyes rebel—
Short-sighted am I or else you suffer from illusions,
    which?—
I do not seem to see these blocks
(I see your geometric palaces)
But only finely powdered stuff
That lends itself to shifting forms and fancies,
I, too, build palaces—
You say they're formless?—
Palaces of gracious curve and shifting color.

The wind and hail and rain cannot harm them,
For they shift of themselves chameleon-like.
It's as you will—
I'd rather work in powder than in blocks.

THE BLIND MAN

Stone blind. That's why they could not fool him.
When they talked to him, he heard the words,
And, more than words, he heard the heart that
    pulsed beneath.
As he sat in his lonely hall of eternal night,
His soul was quick to catch each fleeting nuance
Of the voice, each tell-tale accent lost to seeing ears.
Candor and hypocrisy, like as two peas, he held apart
    as easily
As grain from chaff,
For he was stone blind, and could not be deceived.

THE OLD MAN

Yes, I am old. My sons are grown and wed,
And I am left alone to end my days
In peace and dull content. I've had my fill
Of life and pleasure, too—of love and joy
Of strife and fruits of combat—and a dream
Or two have bathed my daily round in gold,
In misty gold that interposed itself
Between me and the chilly air of fact—
How can one else drag out his days and keep
His heart unseared? But now that age has clung
To me with gently mocking smile (as though
To say, "You cannot shake me off"), I need
No golden mist to shield me. I can see
Unruffled what in younger days might well
Have chilled my ardor, dulled the edge of life,
For now I know that such is naught but sauce
To flavor with its irony the dish
Of life. The vinegar that poisons youth
(And hence in self-defence they dub it wine)
I welcome with the sweet. They call me old,
The young ones, knowingly contend that I
Have lost my step and fallen out of line,
And say I've not the faculty to taste
Their vintages. I say their vintages
Are just the same old liquid (sourish stuff)
We used to sip, but dished in bottles new.
They smile contempt, I answer back with grin
Of "Wait and see." They say I'm way behind
The times; I chuckle "That may be, but you
Run hard! catch up with me and Father Time."

THE MAN OF LETTERS

He had a stock of pretty heirlooms,
Left him by his aunts and grandames, grandames of his aunts, and aunts of grandames.
All his life he played with them and sorted them
And built up pretty patterns out of them,
Graceful and shiny;
Circles, crosses, diamonds, and swastikas he made,
And toyed with shapes refreshingly irregular,
As when he'd dent a kink into a rigid square
And talk of a wayward frolicking Gypsy-like rhythm.
He grew to be exquisitely expert with dainty shapes.
But when he wished to make a solid masterpiece,
He filched a coat or waistcoat from his neighbor,
Strung his trinkets on in circles, crosses, diamonds, and swastikas
And lo! the thing had mass and glitter, too.
"Sublime!" the people said, " 'tis solid matter
Decked with subtle art,"
And lauded most the noble garment underneath.
His right eye slyly winked his left:
"Stick your pretty baubles on your neighbor's coat,
They'll call it yours."

I gave my literary friend a thought.
He made a volume out of it
And now, they say, he sits with Chesterton and Shaw.

THE PROFESSOR

I doubt if you know how wise I am.
Last year I published a heavy tome
Of well-nigh eight-hundred pages.
The subject? It matters not;
But this I know, that only two men in the world
Understood (or partly understood) its learned fill.
One was a spectacled *privat-docent* in Bonn,
The other was myself.
And yet some Philistines begrudge my salary!

THE METAPHYSICIAN

I watched the dog
As he chased his tail
Merrily, merrily round.
Once he thought he had it,
Then he yelped with glee;
But no, he found he was in error,
So had to chase his tail once more
Merrily, merrily round.

I cannot say if he's at it yet—
I left him as busy as ever.

EPITAPH OF A PHILOSOPHER

I had a perfect system when I lived,
Flawless, water-proof to fallacy;
The world but seemed a string of episodes
Each born to prove my system.
Nature and Man and God were each assigned a
    comfortable niche
And Art and Law both fitted like a glove.
But ever since they dug a hole for me,
To meditate in till the further reach of time,
I've thought out many systems more—
One a day's about my average—
And lo! each system fits more perfectly than any
    other.
Of late I've tried to find a system
Unsusceptible of flawless demonstration;
Alas! I have not found one yet.
O gentle tombstone-visitor, have you?

THE CLERGYMAN

I met him in the smoker of a Montreal-bound Pullman.
At first his uncleft collar, separated from a pair of shrewdly twinkling eyes
By energetic chin and Roman nose,
Kept me distant, for I'm not a cleric-fancier.
We were alone, he studying his railroad folder—times of leaving and arriving—
I yawning as I looked for pretty faces in a theatre magazine.
We could not keep it up—
The silence hurt, it dinned so in our ears.
The weather ran the gauntlet first,
The crops and prospects for a ready flow of money
Seemed to occupy us gravely next,
A little politics for entrée brought us to the anecdotal stage.
We got quite chummy, he and I—
Three hours or so we had to let each know
How clever t'other was.
He told some good ones—oh, most proper ones,
But good ones.
My wares he sampled like a connoisseur—
Shrieking with laughter when 'twas safe,
Rocking back and forth,
Slapping his hands down on his knees;
And when 'twas safe, but not so safe,
He laughed again but did without the shrieking, rocking, slapping;
And when you could not call it safe (according to the parlor code),

He smiled an angel's smile and, in the manner of a
    lightning-rod,
He told one of his own,
A good one—O, most proper,
But still a good one.
He had an endless stock, but I soon tired
And turned the talk to church.
There, too, his fund was inexhaustible:
Statistics, Red Cross benefits, a hundred shifts to
    interest the young,
Amateur theatricals and lectures on the Eskimo,
All these and much besides he spoke of with au-
    thority.
We passed the time most entertainingly.
The train pulled into town;
We parted friends, exchanging cards and club ad-
    dresses.
I hurried to the office, thinking him over.
"Good sort," I mused, "a human chap,
As human as they make them;
Leaves his religious dope at home when up against
    a man."
And then I wondered for a second
(I'd reached the office building, had no time to
    bother thinking),
"Does he leave religious dope at home
When up against his crowd in church?"

THE LEARNED JEW

His learning was a many-chambered treasure-house.
He knew the Sabbath and the week-day rituals by heart
And in a trice could mumble off in prayer a dozen pages
Of the closest printed type, while thinking of his slender weekly gains.
He knew the Pentateuch by heart and freely used its wordy commentators
To salt the *bon-mots* of his daily life.
Did you dare to quote a passage from the sacred book—
Anywhere from Genesis to Chronicles (the Hebrew version has them last)—
And slur a vowel or misplace a prefixed article,
Beware! he'd pounce upon you, smile contempt, and make you feel a fumbling school-boy;
He'd clean forget the reverence due a well-filled pocket-book—
Money's a thing of earth, philology's a thing of God!

The Talmud was his favorite picnic-ground;
Give him a heavy tome (one of the Babylonian set)
Wherein the cryptic Aramaic text is swallowed
In the enormous welter of the Hebrew glosses, exegesis, disputatious hairlet-splitting,
Give him this and three or four long-bearded disputants
To wrestle with him for the uttermost possession of the law divine
(By aid of frenzied gestures and an intonation sliding recklessly from roof to cellar),

Give him this and let him split a split hair finer yet
(Sometimes he'd catch the Rabbi napping, bowl him
    over with an exegetic point),
And he was happier than any hobby-riding child.
The Talmud was his dreamland refuge from the
    world.

What was his outward shell? What met the Gentile's eye?
Why, merely this: he kept a peanut stand on Hester
    Street.

THE WOMAN ON THE BRIDGE

I passed her on the bridge;
Her image is with me yet,
And I shall not soon forget
The sadness of her face.

I shall not soon forget
Her pinched and haggard face;
I would I could erase
The memory of her eyes,

Her eyes that empty stared
Into an empty air,
Her eyes that did not dare
To look at what they saw.

And her thin and bony frame
And the narrow chest so flat—
But her eyes, her eyes, 'twas that
That I cannot forget.

O Lord, her eyes have bored
Themselves into my soul,
The've bored themselves a hole
Into my aching heart.

I have not seen her since,
I do not know her tale,
But this I know without fail,
Her life is misery.

TO A MAIDEN SWEET AND PURE

Yes, you are sweet and pure;
Your eyes are calm and open,
Looking straight at me without a blink.
Your hair is neatly parted,
Neatly braided and beribboned.
Your lips are parted daintily,
Your teeth—I'd call them pearls,
Were not the praise so hackneyed.
And your smile is very pleasant to behold,
Bright and sunny.
And all about you floats an air of purity
So fresh, it were most base to blow the wind of
    passion.

Ah me, you're charming, girl, and very sweet,
And yet there's want in you of still more charm.
And shall I tell you why?
But then you must not look at me so open-eyed,
So straight at me without a blink.
I would your eyes were stormier,
I would they gave a hint of ruffled waters under-
    neath;
I would about your head there rayed
A silky aureole of saucy straying hair,
Not quite so neatly prisoned;
I would your pearly teeth were strung
Not quite so motionless between your daintily parted
    lips;
And most of all I would your smile
Were sunny warmth instead of sunny light alone.
I would not have your purity less fresh and pure,
I would but have it crown a glowing maidenhood,
Not merely grace a perfect calm;
I would, you maiden sweet and pure,
I would some hidden yearning
Were mirrored well nigh imperceptibly
In your sweet countenance.

THE STENOGRAPHER

The minutes lengthen into hours, the hours stretch out to days,
Day follows day, day follows day.
Hour after hour I click the typewriter
And grind out words and words and yet more words.
Sometimes I cramp my fingers round a pencil
And set it racing o'er the pad
In swift obedience to my boss's voice,
I let it dance a headlong dance of splashing dribbling strokes—
These, too, are words and words and yet more words.

Sometimes I'm all alone,
Sometimes the fingers droop, forgetful of their task,
Leaving my thoughts to roam unfettered in a garden,
To climb a hillock and to spy the distant land.
The land is covered with a mist,
Warm and palpitating;
And from its bosom floats to me a fragrance that intoxicates,
And flames leap forth,
Aud luring sounds are wafted to me
And sometimes I catch a syllable or two
That make me blush with pleasure and with shame.
But sometimes from the bosom of the mist
Come cooling breezes, honey-laden,
That play about my head and brush caresses on my hair
And leave their honey on my lips and on my drowsy eyes.

"O land of mist, O land of hope, O land of wild desire!
What have you, blessed flaming land, in store for me?"

Sometimes my thoughts unfettered in a garden roam,
Yet not to tarry long.
A moment jolts me back to stare at keyboard and the letter still unfinished;
Then there's "As per your order of the 7th" and all the rest of it to do.—
You see, I do not always click the typewriter,
I do not always dash the pencil on its dancing course.

TO A RECRUITING GIRL

Silly girl!
Urge him not on to slaughter and to sacrifice of
 self
With your reproachful eyes,
With your scornful beauty.
Let him wrestle with himself
And see the light
As 'tis given him to see—
To kill or spare,
To die or live.

Silly girl!
Why desecrate his struggle,
Why pour into his agony of soul
The fiery drop of sex
To goad him on?
Let him crucify himself!
Nail him not to the cross!
And you?
Tremble!
Cast your eyes downward to the earth
In awe that men their own destruction will.
Look not at him brazenly—
Like a wanton.

PROFESSORS IN WAR-TIME

Ho, professors, lend a hand!
Stand not aloof
And wisely smile
While all the world is soaked in blood and groans
    with pain.
You know the reasons for it all—
Do you?—
The tangled web of cause and effect
That strains and pulls and tightens
Till it has the world caught in its hellish grip,
Fly-fashion in a spider's web;
You know the why and how.
Perchance you can distil from all the histories, dis-
    quisitions, encyclopædias
That you have writ and read
Some kindly counsel or ray of hope
To loose the web.
Let your owlish smile thaw out
Into the human glance of human kind.
Ho, professors, lend a hand
And help us out of hell!

HOW DIPLOMATS MAKE WAR

Have you ever seen a picture of an ancient
House on piles deep-driven in a lake?
They used to live in them in old Helvetia
For safety's sake—at least I'm told as much by
    archæologists.

Well, I saw one used myself—it's now a bit more
    than two years ago—
A great big house all full of people—men and
    women
And young ones, too.
My, you'd think they never knew they had but
Rotten timbers 'twixt them and death—
They seemed so gay and unconcerned and safe!

And then I saw a crowd of boys amuse themselves
    on land
At throwing stones—
Great big stones they threw in rivalry.
At first it seemed to me they pelted one the other,
But no! they aimed their shots
Straight at the piles that held the house,
And all the while they laughed and cried with glee—
Such sport it was.
The dwellers in the house looked on—
And they, too, laughed and cried with glee,
For the piles were strong—no need to fear.

And by and by the boys to the uttermost
Strained themselves.
They yelled and cried with fury, for none would
    be outdone;

They hurled great boulders they could barely lift,
Hurled them headlong at the piles.
The dwellers in the house looked on—
And they, too, yelled and cried with fury,
For each one bet on his favorite boy.

They of the house egged on the throwers of stones,
Who lashed themselves to greater fury, for none
      would be outdone.
The stones went whirling thick,
So thick they nearly hid the piles,
One could not see the budging of the piles,
One could not hear them bend and creak.

In a trice the piles gave way,
I saw the house tip and come with a splash.
It spilled the people.
They sprawled and fought for life,
And many drowned.
But the boys kept up their heated yells
And quarreled bravely—
They quarreled bravely on dry land.

EPITAPH OF A SOLDIER

I died for king and native land,
I died for justice and the right,
But most of all I died because a shell
Just caught me in the nick of time
And finished me.

THE OLD MAID AND THE PRIVATE

He had come home on a furlough,
Left hand in a sling, his right leg cut away;
He'd seen some bayonet work at Neuve Chapelle,
His mutilated self, astir on crutch, bore witness to
    the music he had heard.
They called him hero.
His maiden aunts and a whole bevy of maiden
    friends of maiden aunts
Lionized him to their hearts' content,
Lionized him till he yawned with boredom.
Now one old maid addressed herself to him
With ardent patriotism.
In accents stern and threatening
She spewed her venom on the hated Boches,
She burned their wicked bodies in a Hell
That made th' Inferno of Alighieri look like Para-
    dise.

Oh the Germans,
Oh the dastard sons of Beelzebub,
Oh fiendish hosts of evil!
Where is the cruel death that would not be a
    mercy to them,
Where the torture smacking not of meek forgive-
    ness?

No quarter! no quarter!
And her eyes blazed a thousand lights—
One saw she had been beautiful in days gone by.

The private listened dutifully,
Coughed a little cough and fidgeted about.
This atmosphere was very tense, he thought.
"Oh well," after a bit he meekly interposed,
"The Kaiser, he's a bad one, sure enough.
But these here common chaps,
They're pretty much the same as me and all the
    rest of us—
Pretty decent chaps, you know,
That kill and die,
Just do as they are told.
I wouldn't stick a bayonet into one
If I could help it, that's a fact;
Some prisoners I've known
Are jolly fine, now that's another."

"Impossible!" she snapped,
Her eyes "No quarter!" blazed.
"I'd crush them all like vermin,
Stick them till they bleed to death like hogs!"
"Maybe," he said, "but, then, you women-folk have
    got us beat
On spunk. We've no such bravery."

DELILAH

Did you say you're strong?
Did you say your will is free to loose and break?
Did you vaunt your precious brain,
Cunning weaver of a gossamer web of beautiful
    dreams,
Cunning weaver of an intricate maze of truth?

But I am stronger than you.
Your will to loose and break is fettered when I
    will.
Your precious brain is slave to me,
For than your beautiful dreams more beautiful
    am I,
And than your maze of truth more true is my
    treacherous self.

For you are the ice,
And I am the sun that melts the ice.
For you are the cold,
And I am the heat that kills the cold.
For you are the colorless glass,
And I am the glow that suffuses the colorless glass
    with a radiant hue.
For you are mind,
And I am the passion that burns the mind.

I have but to pour the light of my beautiful eyes
On your starving face,
And you are my slave.
I have but to dazzle your eyes
With the dazzling light and the clinging warmth
    of my beautiful smiles,
And you are my slave.

I have but to shower my glistening knee-long tresses
    of black
On your hungering face,
And you are my slave.
I have but to clasp my shining arms about you,
And I have but to press my bosom against your
    throbbing heart,
And I have but to press my lips on your thirsty lips,
And you are my utter slave.

For you are the stone,
And I am the fire that cracks the stone.
For you are the tree,
And I am the flame that chars the tree.
For you are longing,
And I am the laughing maiden that lures and ca-
    resses and tortures.
For you are desire,
And I am the love that meets desire.

THE REPORTER CONGRATULATES THE ORATOR

Yes, sir, I heard your speech.
'Twas wonderful to sail along the sunlit flow
Of words that gently streamed into my ear,
To glide like passive twig from swirl to eddy in
    the current.
You held us captive for an hour—
Two hours, no doubt, you might have platform-
    chained our eyes and ears—
And generaled our thoughts and sentiments to march
    with yours.
How did you do it?
I ask because my paper wants a column of report
In summary. I've struggled hard this hour
Or more to get the gist of what you said—
Just gist—on paper;
Bah! I can't do better, sir, than three poor miserable
    lines.

THE PAINTING

He wove a color-fabric out of paint
That warmed the heart,
He poured out light upon his canvas
Till the eye was drunk with delight.
Spots and streaks he dealt out recklessly,
And when he'd finished—
See! a perfect vision sunned itself before you.
They looked at it and asked,
"What does it mean?"
He mumbled in reply,
"A little louder, please.
I cannot hear;
My ears are not as long as yours."

The Dainty Man

I offer you sweet cakes, a thousand tasty morsels
To tickle your palate.
Eat and rejoice.

The Hungry Man

No. Your sweets disgust me.
I crave a rougher fare.
I'll try my teeth on coarse bread—husks and all.
I want the stuff of brawn and muscle, the stuff
    that life is made of.

The Dainty Man

And let me show you my flower garden of languor-
    ous, intoxicating perfumes.
Each breath shall be to you a sheer delight.
You shall inhale the haunting violet, the enervating
    rose, the teasing mint.

The Hungry Man

No. Your perfumes choke me.
Give me the salt-laden tang of the ocean, the scent
    of horses' dung,
And the odor of smouldering leaves.
I would not shun the stench of the slums, for there
    is life.

The Dainty Man

And your ears I shall fill with splendid sonorities,
With the liquid warblings of flutes and the gentle boomings of kettle-drums.
The harmonious hum of happy voices shall fill your ears.

The Hungry Man

I would not be lulled.
I want my ears to tingle with shouts and with shrieks.
The thunderbolt and the creaking of ungreased axles
Must thrill me.
And my ears strain to catch the whispers of the night.

The Dainty Man

Come, see the rainbow arched o'er the earth,
See the glowing tints merge.
Would not your eyes feast on the setting sun,
And flutter at the fluttering wings of the humming-bird?

The Hungry Man

Rather the tangled green and gray of the forest,
Rather the tangled motley crowds in the street.
My eye roams through the thick of life;
My eye seeks the dancing feet and the rows of tenements,
The sunlight peeping into alleys and the palace bathed in fog.

The Dainty Man

I bring you many joys, subtle and rare;
I shall soothe your troubled heart with lovely images
And with thoughts serene.
The world I shall make for you into a lovely and
    serene abode.

The Hungry Man

But the joy unmingled with pain is as death to me.
And more to me than thoughts serene are the striv-
    ings and turmoils of the heart,
And more to me than lovely images is the wayward
    current of life.
I seek no abode;
I desire to thread life's mazes in the open.

The Dainty Man

Then take to yourself a faith,
Or you will lose your way.

The Hungry Man

I want no leading strings.
Here and there, and then and now,
I must be equally at home on the earth.

The Dainty Man

I distil from the crassness of life
What matters alone—Beauty.
Take it.

The Hungry Man

What matters alone to me—it is Life,
The crassness of life.

THE WATER NYMPH

She

When did you love me first?

He

When first I saw you, dear.

She

A year ago in June
Out at the farm? Your eyes
Had not been set on me
Before.

He

   O yes, they had.
I'd seen your beauty clear
As morning dew. I'd seen
Your golden locks unloosed
Caressing your white breasts;
I'd seen them fall to kiss
Your body, dear.

She

No!

He

Yes,
You cannot know, but shall
I tell you how it was?—
I'd gone to seek, one morn
In early spring, a still
Retreat far out from town
Along the river's bank,
A fav'rite nook of mine,
Where bittern's cry and splash
Of wild ducks scarce could break
The peaceful calm. I'd gone
To laze around and read
In quiet—it's a way
Of mine when tired of folks—
Perhaps to throw a line
And pull a fish or two
Besides. The spot is down
By Hunter's Bend, right close
To swirling cataracts,
But there's a pool this side
That's off the channel, safe
And deep—a splendid spot
For swim or dive; I've tried
It once or twice myself.

She

Down by the alder clump
Between the narrow beach
And grassy swale?

He

      Just where
I'd dozed away, when splash!
"Some one's just jumped to dive,"
I thought, awakened.

She

        Oh!
To think I'd come miles out
To have my little plunge
In freedom, just to fall
A prey to prying eyes!

He

Sh! don't call it that,
My love. I thought at first
To hail the diver, but
Before I'd time to rise,
He'd come out from the pool.
The "he" was you. So dazed
Was I, I stared and took
You for a water-nymph—
And so you are.

She

     For shame!
Why could not you have left?

He

How could I, dear? The dry,
Dead leaves that Fall had strewn
Had crackled if I'd stirred,
And whipped a flood of red
Into your face. I could
But lie and hold my breath
And trust you would not know.

She

You could have looked away.

He

And so I could. But, Oh,
You were too beautiful,
My love; you were my nymph,
My lovely water-nymph
So fair. Your golden hair
Caressed your bosom white
And played with sunbeams bright.
You were so beautiful and pure,
So like a goddess free,
I could have worshipped you
And kissed your little feet
A-glist'ning in the sun.
And ever since you've been
To me the water-nymph.

She

And that was why you blushed
And stared so stupidly
When first you met me—no!
When first I met you?

He

      Yes,
For you were not a girl
Of human kind to me;
You were my water-nymph
So beautiful and free,
Whose golden hair caressed
Your bosom white, the nymph
Whose little pearl-shod feet,
A-glist'ning in the sun,
I could have kissed.

She

      And so
I gave myself to you
Before I knew you!

He

      No,
My love, say rather I
Was yours before I learned
To know your human form.
And if you ask me when
It was I loved you first,
I'll say I loved you first
In early spring, the time
I met the water-nymph.

CURTAINS.

I enter the Chinaman's laundry;
And the merry queer-voiced gabbing,
That hops about while the flat-irons slide on the wash,
Ceases. The three are as mum as shining door-knobs,
And rock as they stand in their places,
Clattering their slippers on the floor
And pressing and sliding their flat-irons on the wash.
My fingers fumble in my pocket for the ticket,
And my nostrils breathe the steamy air,
And the Chinaman that shines most like a darkly burnished door-knob
Shuffles to the counter.
Patiently he stares a nascent smile.
I find the black-daubed scrap of red and give it him.
He shuffles to the rows of creamy parcels,
Buttoned each with black-daubed scrap of red,
And runs my ticket right to left and left to right and up and down
To find its jagged edge a match.
Ah! two scraps of red mate happily,
The black daubs torn apart by the Chinaman's decree
Now kiss reunion for a moment.
Must be my parcel! Romance has its uses.
"Fi'ty sick!" says he and shoves the creamy bundle on the counter.
"Fifty-six?"—"Fi'ty sick!"
Two quarters and a dime clink on the counter,
Four coppers take their exit from a coin-filled box.
While pocketing my change, I look at him,

And patiently he stares a nascent smile,
While the others clatter their slippers on the floor
And slide the flat-irons on the wash.
"Nice day."—"Yeh, belly waum!"
To the tune of "Fi'ty sick!"
But when I've closed the door,
I hear their queer-voiced gabbing
Burst forth merrily and hop in the air.
For when I enter, the curtain falls and the play
    halts,
And when I leave, the curtain rises and the play
    resumes.

Lucy and I pass honeyed nothings back and forth
On the balcony
And weave the ancient ageless web of romance,
Each wrapped in each.
But when he comes to join us,
The honeyed nothings flee.
For when we're two,
The curtain's up and the play is on,
But when we're three,
The curtain's down and the play is hushed.

MY BOY

There! way off yonder near the farther end
Of the vacant lot—
See the little bobbing patch of brown
Surmounted by a darkish speck?
That's my little boy, brown-jerseyed
And capped with sailor blue.
Look! his little legs rock side to side
As, chased by reddish patch—
That's Jack, his little friend that lives across the
      way from us—
He runs and shrieks with laughter.
Hear him? His voice is higher-pitched than Jack's,
Ripples merrier and brighter (don't you think?).
Oh, there he trips and sprawls—
Not quite as steady on his pins as might be,
But, then, he's only four. And now
He's rolling in the sand yelling splitting peals,
While Jack bombards him with more sand.
She'll have a job to-night, his mother,
To oust the sand-grains from his curly hair,
And I shall threaten him with barber's shears
For making such a nuisance of himself.
Yes, that's my boy.
Well, we must be going to the office—
Can't stand forever gaping at the youngster.
I'll have enough to do in the evening
When, home again, I do his bidding.
I'll have to swing him, lift him to the ceiling,
Tell him the story of the bear and wolf
(I've told him that a hundred times at least,
But it's his favorite—and if I stray in my recital
From the version he has fixed as orthodox,
He'll shout a protest), and, worst of all,

I'll have to tell him why is this, and what is that,
And what did Jack mean when he said "Oh, cut it
　　out!"
"Don't use such words, my boy," I've told him time
　　and time again,
But what's the use? (I do it more
To make his mother think I'm educating him.)
He had the laugh on me the other day—
He was as mulish as could be at table
And when I, all out of patience, yelled at him,
"Now, cut that out!" he gravely turned to me
And asked, "Can daddies say such words?
Why can they? tell me," but I changed the subject
While I helped him to a piece of cake.
It's far from easy, Bob, to do the right thing
With an urchin—quite a strain.
Yes, that was he out in the lot,
My little boy. I bet he's all one sandy mess!

DANDELIONS

He stood upon the porch, my little boy,
And proudly held aloft the dandelions
That he had gathered all himself. "Put these
In water, keep them in a glass," he said.
(Behind him, mellowed to a golden sparkle,
Lazy stirred the pond beneath the wind's
Caress. Two ducks quacked answer to a crow
That, lighting on a maple, cawed a Sunday
Yawn.) The wind drove silky threads of hair
Down on his face—they seemed the little stems
That held his golden smile like dangling flowers
Merged into one. I took the dandelions
And, thankful for the other flower, I thanked
Him for his gift, while off he ran for more.

THE OTHER SIDE

In childhood days I often hearkened
Admiringly to bugle call of postman
Rushing in at golden dusk
In his parcel-laden wagon to the open court
Whereon the post-house gave.
I lived right next the post-house,
That to my childish eyes
Reared itself up proudly and impregnably
Like thick-walled castle turreted in rugged strength.
No unimportant part the post-house
Seemed of my world of romance,
Scarce second to the storks,
Grave emissaries from a mystic land.

One day the little town was all agog
With an elbowing crowd to see a fire.
The stir and strange alarums frightened me,
But most of all that day has fixed itself for ever
On the tablet of my mind because the castellated
 post-house
Transformed itself into a longish windowed thing
 of brick.
The maid that minded me,
Lured like the rest by the magic of a burning house,
Held me by the hand and led me to the crowd,
Led me to a street I ne'er had tramped.
It seemed another world, had not the kindly look
Of street and alley known to me;
And yet 'twas but a mere stone's throw from where
 I lived
And gazed upon the post-house walls.
She took me through the post-house gate
Into the court and then—

I held my breath as we adventured boldly—
Right through the mighty building
Out to the other entrance leading to the street
The crowd was on, the street I ne'er had seen.
Strange! I'd never thought the post-house had two
    sides,
And as it now betrayed itself an unfamiliar longish
    bit of windowed brick,
My heart was troubled.
So might a friend you'd known for years
In a moment of ill-considered act or word
Of a sudden reveal himself a stranger.
I could not reconcile myself to think this unknown
    line of red
Hearkened with me to the bugle call at golden dusk;
I would not let it share in the romance I had built
Out of the side I knew—my side.

'Tis well we know but one side of our souls,
The side that looks out on the open court of self,
The side that's glamor-tinted.
'Tis well we cannot call our own the other side,
The bit of brick that fronts the world
And marks us for our neighbors.
I thank God that I cannot penetrate the walls of the
    soul
And see the me that's seen by you.

MUTUAL UNDERSTANDING

My dog and I, we get on very well—
Oh, very well, indeed. We understand
Each other perfectly, you see. Each swish
Of his stubby tail, each upward pleading look,
Each choppy yelp or squirmy growl, is clear
To me as any word of man; it needs
No speech confirmatory of its meaning.
Delight and hunger, shame, repentance, all
The joys and pains and mental conflicts known
Of man my dog makes dumbly clear to me.
I read him like a book—no, like a man.
I bother not with dog psychology,
But treat him like a man of doggish look
And habits. Works well, anyhow. We've not
A quarrel had as yet (far more than I
Can say of any man or woman known
To me). I think he treats me just the same
Mutatis mutandis, I mean he seems to look
On me as psychologically dog,
Just outwardly a man; and when I wrinkle
My brow or read a book, I'm sure he thinks
I'm busied with some doggishly correct
Intelligible act or thought—at least
His look is all approval. So—the moral—
By misinterpreting each other wholly
And scorning speech, two souls can easiest
In mutual understanding live. How lucky
I have no knowledge of the barking code
Or cut of doggish soul! How lucky, too,
He's never learned to talk nor studied James'
Psychology! For then I doubt if we
Could quite so sympathetically chum.

A CONVERSATION

You sit before me and we talk
Calmly and unafraid.
Calmly and unafraid
I sink my net into your soul,
That flows before me like a limpid stream.
I draw forth many lovely things
That you had thought were hid;
I draw forth many ugly things
That you had thought were pure,
That you had never thought to hide.

THE DREAMER FAILS OF SUCCESS

You and I started off for the mountain top
Clad in snow, standing out
Clear and strong in the light,
Clear and bold o'er the land.

You went straight to the mark,
Over the fields and across the brooks and past the
    bushes and all,
You never strayed from the road
Lengthening straight over hill and plain,
You never halted nor rested to gladden your eyes
With the sunbeam's play or the butterfly's merry-go-
    round,
But on you pressed, tireless,
Intent, strung,
Until you reached the mountain top
Clad in snow. But you were too spent
To stand out clear and strong in the light
And look about you.

But as for me, I could not stick to the road
That led to the white-clad mountain top.
Once I threw me down on the grass,
Face to the sky,
And gazed on the heavy-sailing clouds,
Pondering their fantastic forms
And giving them names
And wondering whence they came and whither they
  went
Unerringly, like sail-boats
Languidly gliding along on a calm blue sea;
And I saw the tops of the fir trees high above me
Gently nodding back and forth,
And suddenly it seemed they were camel's-hair
  brushes
Writing a language of signs on the sky,
And the signs that they wrote were
Heavy-sailing clouds in fantastic forms;
And as I gazed in the sky and lost the hang of all
  that was near,
I seemed to float on air and I seemed somehow
To bend the firs to my will and to make them
  write my dreams
On the sky, and the dreams that they wrote were
Heavy-sailing clouds in fantastic forms.

Once I strayed from the road and came to a great
  salt lake.
'Twixt the lake and the sky
There circled many gulls
Cleaving paths for themselves with wing-flaps strong
  and sure;
Once in a while a gull would soar aloft and make
  for the sky,
Only to fall to a lower track in the air,

And once in a while a gull would fly out of sight,
    swift and low,
Only to circle back to its starting point;
And as the aerial tracks of the gulls lengthened and
    shortened
And criss-crossed back and forth,
It seemed to me that the gulls were quickly sailing
    kites
Moored to strings that lengthened and shortened;
And as I gazed in the air and lost the hang of all
    that was near,
I seemed to hold the strings in my hands and fly
    the kites as I willed,
For the kites were my thoughts and desires
That circled restlessly
And aspired to heights and far-off distances,
Only to fall again in their wonted tracks.

And so I lazed along the road and off
And made the whole world mine.
I never reached the mountain top
Clad in snow. Yet I would not change with you,
For what can one see from the mountain top
That I have not seen on the road and off?

DISCORDS

Dearest friend, I pray you for silence.
I know you mean to banish sorrow from my mind,
Exorcising with your cheery voice, recounting cheerful things.
O friend, have mercy!

You cannot annihilate the stream that winds through my soul,
Mournful and sluggish under the brooding willows;
You can but force your rippling torrent, racing garrulously,
Into the middle channel of my stream,
But the waters mingle not,
And my soul is tortured by the flowing side by side
Of incommensurable rhythms.
You cannot hush the sombre-tinted line of music,
Harmonized in minor chords,
That drifts on the current of my soul;
You can but lay upon my strand your garish line of music,
Harmonized in major chords,
But these two strands refuse to spin themselves into a weft,
But each drifts hostile on the current of my soul.
(You know that mingled major chord and minor
Torture the ear with a dissonance
Excruciating like the sawing of a nail.)

Silence, friend,
I pray you—dearest friend!
In the friendly silence perhaps the sluggish stream will seep away

In time, leaving the willows high and dry
And thirsting for your rippling torrent.
In the friendly silence perhaps the sombre-tinted
 strains will die into inaudible mist
In time, leaving the current of my soul
Free to float your garish strand.
But meanwhile
Silence, silence,
Dearest friend, I pray you—
For it is not merry in my soul.

LOVE

I'd read of it and dreamt of it
And longed for it;
I'd thought it must be chivalrous and vast
And nobly heaven-storming,
The word had set my thoughts on knights
And valiant combat, humble worship,
Lily smiles received in ecstasy.
But now I know it's more than this, far more,
And you have taught me, love.
It means that when your little feet come tripping,
A symphony floods in my ears;
It means that when I run my fingers through your
 hair,
I cannot see for happiness.

OUR LOVE

Our love is singing, dear,
Full-throated,
Rising drunk with joyous passion,
And carolling, carolling
Madly in its abandoned flight
Upward, ever upward,
Cloudward, my beloved,
Skyward, my radiant blessed love.

Our love is trembling, dear,
Deep-glowing
Like golden sunbeam darkened in red wine,
And warming, warming
Our hearts like golden light that warms our hair,
Illumining our eyes with passion,
Warming, my beloved,
Burning, my radiant blessed love.

Our love is trembling, dear,
Deep-throbbing
In its ecstasy of happiness,
And weeping, weeping
Shyly, blissfully,
Overcome with the choking fulness of its joy,
Trembling, my beloved,
Trembling, my radiant blessed love.

DANGLING CORPSES

I know that which livelier
Shakes in the wind
Than the noisy shutters down the street.
I know that which merrier
Swings in the wind
Than the flaming banners down the street.
I know a monstrous presence
O'ershadowing the life
That simmers on the street.
I see the corpse erect
That dangles from the gallows' head,
That shakes and swings in the wind
And casts a shadow.

Upon the laughter and the bustle of your soul's
    domain
There falls no shadow of a corpse
Dangling from a grinning past?
Thrice blessed!

TO DEBUSSY

"La Cathédrale Engloutie"

Like a faint mist, murkily illumined,
That rises imperceptibly, floating its way nowhence, nowhither,
Now curling into some momentary shape, now seeming poised in space—
Like a faint mist that rises and fills before me
And passes;

Like a vague dream, fitfully illumined,
That wanders irresponsibly, flowing unbid nowhence, nowhither,
Now flashing into a lurid flame-lit scene, now seeming lost in haze—
Like a vague dream that lights up and drifts within me
And passes;

So passes through my ear the memory of the misty strain,
So passes through my mind the memory of the dreamy strain.

DIRTY SPRING

The streets are filled with muck,
A dirty mess of melting snow and mud,
Splashing recklessly
As heavy-footed horses trot along.
Down from the snow-encrusted roofs
An icy dirty trickle pelts the pavement,
Little splashes mid the universal splash.
And the sky is blotched with dirty-gray cloudlets
Speeding under the sun.
The porches dribble with wet and they gently
    steam
Where the sun, piercing the dirty cloudlets,
Can cook them.
An irritated wind blows intermittently,
Banging doors, scattering wisps, flapping capes and
    skirts.

The snow-locked beauty of winter is gone,
The rigors are loosening up;
Clean summer's not here yet.
The city moves from cleanly cold to cleanly warmth
Immersed in dirt.

Therefore, my friends, take heart!
You must not despair
When the passage from old to new is dirty;
When you've left the old realm of glittering cold
And have not yet reached the new realm of glisten-
    ing warmth;
When dead tradition is back of you,
When the new-born promise is off ahead of you,
And you struggle and splash in a welter of mud.

AN EASTER DAY

'Tis Easter day to-day!
And what a day for rendering jubilant thanks
To him who made the day!

The snow has melted off the streets,
That now smile in the sun,
Dry and clean.
How pure they seem in the sun and the rugged
    wind,
How pure they seem under the purer sky!
The sky is but a rind of blue
Set o'er a vast and gleaming world of light,
The world a blue-surmounted temple
Shouting joy and thundering thankfulness
To him who made the day;
And in this thundering thankfulness
I hear a thousand voices vibrant with joy.
I hear the peeping sparrows as they fidget
About the leafless trees;
I hear the rugged wind blow lustily;
I hear the timid blades of grass recite their matins,
Promising to cloak the earth with green;
And most of all I hear the blazing light
Poured earthward by the sun,
Trumpet back a thundering thankfulness
To him who made the day.

I, too, would drown my voice among the thousand
    voices
Thundering thankfulness, vibrant with joy,
And so I let my steps ring out
Triumphant on the blue-surmounted temple's floor
And mount in thankfulness

To him who made the day.
And as I wandered, free as bird and wind,
I met a friend who hurried with a book;
I tried to hold him on the temple's floor
To sing with me a song of jubilant thanks
To him who made the day.
Perhaps the blazing light too loudly trumpeted for him—
He scurried, rabbit-fashion, off into a cross-surmounted house
Where thanks, he said, were offered up to God.

SUMMER IN THE WOODS

The lazy day is humming,
It is drowned in a languid drone,
And I, stretched out in drowsy indolence
Upon the grass, shaded but blotched with sun,
Can feel its lazy heart beat slow and warm
In sympathy with mine.
There is a thickish, honeyed feeling in the air that lulls.

An image vaguely, sluggishly—half dream, half thought—
Begins to separate from out the formless, bundled mass of sense
That veils my soul—
Gone! the wasp has caught it in its buzzing flight
And turned it to a droning revery
That floats off there before me,
Now biting thick into my ear,
Now thinning out into a distant hum.
It's all but melted into the drowsy murmur
That gilds the encompassing silence,

When it lives again as a shy rustling
That has gently stolen on me;
And when I close my eyes, it seems the rustle of
    my soul
In lazy flight and shy,
And when I peer through eyes half-opened at the
    sky,
It seems the whispered confidences of the clouds
    among themselves
As they dally by,
But when I look in mid air,
Then I know it is the leaves fidgeting in the wind.

What is that faintly lapping sound off yonder?
Timidly it seems to wash something.
At first I see but trees huddled darkly—
Then a ribboned little patch of silver
Crushed between the trees and the darker earth.
The river!

BEFORE THE STORM

Evil's in the air.
I feel it throbbing, sighing, twisting all about me
And it presses dull against my heart
And makes my eyes to stare.
Evil whines in the sickening wind
(Like a Chinese stringèd bow
Whining out a plangent strangled jejune tune),
The loathsome wind that drops from the trees
And shivers down my spine.
Evil sits in the gaunt bare forks
Of the dead old oaks
That sway in lazy apathy.
Evil sails through the air
As the greedy crows caw and croak
In their lumbering flight from oak to oak,
In their offal-dropping flight.
And the leaden sky is laden with evil,
With the filthy dirty-moist clouds
That smudge the atmosphere
And dome the smothered earth.
O Lord! crack the air with a thunderbolt
And let me breathe!

A MOONLESS NIGHT

I'm swallowed up in night,
  That, flapping noiselessly his giant bat-wings, hovers motionless.
The blackness penetrates me slowly, slowly,
Till I vanish and am night;
The silence gnaws into me
  Till I hear the noiseless flapping of the giant wings of night.
Up above the stars are not of night;
They do but timorously peep at the void
And, frightened, huddle close and shiver.

THE RAIN

Quickening life-giving rain!
Drench my loosened hair with thy
    tempestuous flood,
Trickling down rivulets that earthward
    plunge,
Eager to kiss my thirsty feet.

O rain, beneficent clinging rain
That splashest headlong down from a
    gray vault,
Embrace my naked body,
Cool its fevered yearning.

Streaming life-giving rain!
Beat strongly on my shoulders,
Burdened with care,
Free them with your cleansing.

O rain, beneficent, whipping rain
That drivest storm-tossed against me,
Play upon my laughing breasts,
Happy to kiss thee, rain.

WATER

Rain and snow and hail and ice,
The river rolling to the sea,
The ocean rolling to the shore—
I think that Nature takes a deal
    of time and space
To have her little say.

Man is artist.
See him put his soul into a drop
    of it
And make a tear!

THE MOTH

Fluttering, fluttering,
A mad white winged speck,
Flitting across my vision
In quick little angular spurts
All jointed into a noiseless flash,
Drab-white like the ghost of a fire-fly
(Should not ghosts of fire-flies flicker by
    day?).
The merest ghost of irritation,
Absent-minded I,
Makes me clap my hands smartly,
And the little moth,
Powdered in a vise,
Clings, nondescript fluff, to my palm.
First the silence of life,
The bang of fate,
Then the silence of death.
Nothing to me.
Anything to God?

HELPLESS REVOLT

I have no respect for what is.
I can not mend and patch,
I can not bend my soul to the twist
That will make it fit with the brutal fact,
That will make it yield to the tyrant world.
My soul stands firm.
It would annihilate all in its rage and build anew,
Rather than bend.
Therefore it breaks, and the brutal fact remains
And the tyrant world wags on.

LIBERTY

No, Liberty, they shall not make you die.
They shall not squeeze you to the wall and choke
     your life out
With all their throttling collectivities and dismal
     efficiency-mongering.
Or even so, will you not slip into the hearts of many,
When the few have thought to down you,
And build in each a fortress bidding defiance
To all their throttling collectivities?

But should they banish you in very truth,
Come take my hand,
We'll off into the woods and live on roots,
We'll climb the inaccessible mountain peaks
And melt the snow for drink.
We'll leave the hogs to fatten in their troughs;
We'll starve to death, perhaps,
But not before we've breathed some air.

DUST

Dust everywhere!
I cannot see things for the dust-forms
Draped about and over them.
I see a sudden gleam leap here,
A flash of steel leap there;
I catch a fleeting hint of rounded forms,—
Then dust again—clouds on clouds.
I struggle through, like vessel ploughing in a fog.

But then—see!
Off there a fire has burnt a circle in the enveloping
    dust
And set your beautiful countenance, my love,
In glowing light that tints the encircling dust
To a luminous halo.
But the farther dust is still a thicket
Where things are turbulently hid.

WINGS

If I had wings to lift me to the moon,
I'd fold them snugly about me and walk my garden
    plot.
My wings are barely strong enough to lift me to the
    hillock's crest;
That is why they flutter towards the sun.

LONELINESS

Vaguely fretful, up and down the lonely streets I walk
And walk with neither aim nor thought, but like a shadow stalk
Along, a sullen restless shadow, lifeless and yet alive,
Not with the life of vigor live, nor life of such as strive.

Fitting comrade of my moody self where'er I go,
The lifeless rain keeps drizzling on drop after drop, and low
And lower hang the sullen clouds, as were they fain to crush
Utterly the starveling life beneath and make it hush.

Love, I think if you were here, I think the streets would ring
With mirth, the shadow'd take a tripping gait and sing
And laugh, and then the rain, the cheerless drizzling rain, would beat
Merrily down, the while the clouds hang lower us to greet.

VEXATION

Vexation rules my soul.
I'd take a keen delight in giving pain,
In stepping on your toes and pinching you and tweaking you,
In lashing you with venomed tongue.
How hard to keep from slapping your face!

How good to see the whole world scowl and squint and sneer!
In passing quickly by a shop,
I glimpsed a silly maiden on the cover of a magazine—
Her parent thought to make her sweetly smile, no doubt,
She only leered a sickly smirk.

I looked up at the moon.
The smiling man in the moon they talk about
Is all a myth, I saw.
He looked at me and scowled as though to split his crinkled face,
And if he'd had a mouth,
He would have spit on the earth, I know.

What a jaded air the houses have!
The snarling dogs and ugly yawning cats
Slink in the shadows;
Had I the time to stop and fool with them,
I'd pull their tails and kick them hard.
And what a miserable stew
Of scowling, squinting, sneering men
And leering, simpering women—
This aimless crowd I jostle through!

'Tis good to live, you say?
Why, yes, 'tis good to live to see them
Make a sorry mess of living.
Show me a happy man!
I'll box his ears.

SNARED

Ensnared on earth,
The soul in pain did tumble restlessly from
    place to place.
It found no peace.
They would not let it rest and contemplate
In longing calm the home it strayed from,
They would not let it skyward gaze.
And when it sought a moment's solace on a
    mountain peak
Beyond the din of matter,
Unseen powers pulled it down and choked it
In a fume-filled pit.
It tumbled cheerlessly from place to place;
It would have skyward flown
But that they held it snared on earth.
It gasped for breath, yet could not die.
And so it tumbled, tumbled, tumbled on the
    earth.

THE SOUL

Lo! I am many.
There are many chambers in my soul
With windows looking out from one to other.
You cannot hold me.
If you seize me here,
Lo! I am fled and laugh at you from there.

Sometimes I sit in a room of state,
Severely girt with pillars high and marble-white;
Herein I muse on principles, ideals, morals,
Herein I plan to build the starward way
That leads to God.
But if you knock, thinking to find me in,
Lo! I am gone,
Off to the chamber of stormy desires,
Where passions rule,
Where I can gorge myself with appetites and lusts.
You knock and enter in the room begirt with pillars high
And converse hold with a shadow left behind to mock at you.
My poor deluded friend,
Can you not hear your discourse grave
Answered with derisive peals from the seat of revelry?
Perhaps it's just as well you're deaf.

I have a room where angels sing,
Where many instruments make melody;
Here all the air is vibrant with celestial harmonies.
Here sorrow turns to joy,
Here joy's serenity.

I have a room where hammers ring,
Where all is stir and bustle;
Sometimes it pleases me to make a racket,
Nailing planks.

I have a room that's littered o'er with books
And maps and measuring rods;
Sometimes it pleases me to ask a question here or two
And set to work to find an answer.

There is a room I often fancy,
When, tired of star-quest, lusts, reposeful melody,
Tired of labor and inquiry,
I sink in easy-chair and feel a joyous life-force course
Within my veins and long for—what?
I cannot tell.
Accepting all, rejecting all, I long for the unknown,
I long for realms never traversed,
For realms that shall ne'er be traversed.

And many other chambers in my soul there are—
I do not know them all.
There are some dungeons too that frighten me;
You cannot enter these—
I've thrown the keys away.
I like my odd ramshackle house with its countless
    rooms;
I like to flit about, an Ariel, from room to room
And fool you.
If you seize me here,
Lo! I am fled and laugh at you from there.
For I am many.

A PRAYER FOR PRESERVATION

O Lord, preserve my soul;
Teach me to glory in its flight.
And make it strong,
Like the flaming red of the western sky
That stares triumphant at the murky east,
Like the storm-cloud that flashes and dins;
And make it light,
That it wing aloft
And shake itself free of the pressing weight
Of other souls;
And make it unafraid,
That it fear not the tortures of Hell
Or the thrills of dizzy heights
Or the choking mud of the depths;
And make it indifferent,
That it hear not flattery
And laugh at hate
And amuse itself mightily with the taunts
Of other souls;
And make it proud,
That it despise itself
And scorn the bribes of the blaspheming ones
Who call themselves thy priests.

O Lord, preserve my soul;
Let it not perish in the cuddling warmth
That kills all souls
But those that have thy blessing, Lord.

CPSIA information can be obtained at www.ICGtesting.com
Printed in the USA
238188LV00003B/252/P